TRANSPORTATION ADVENTURES

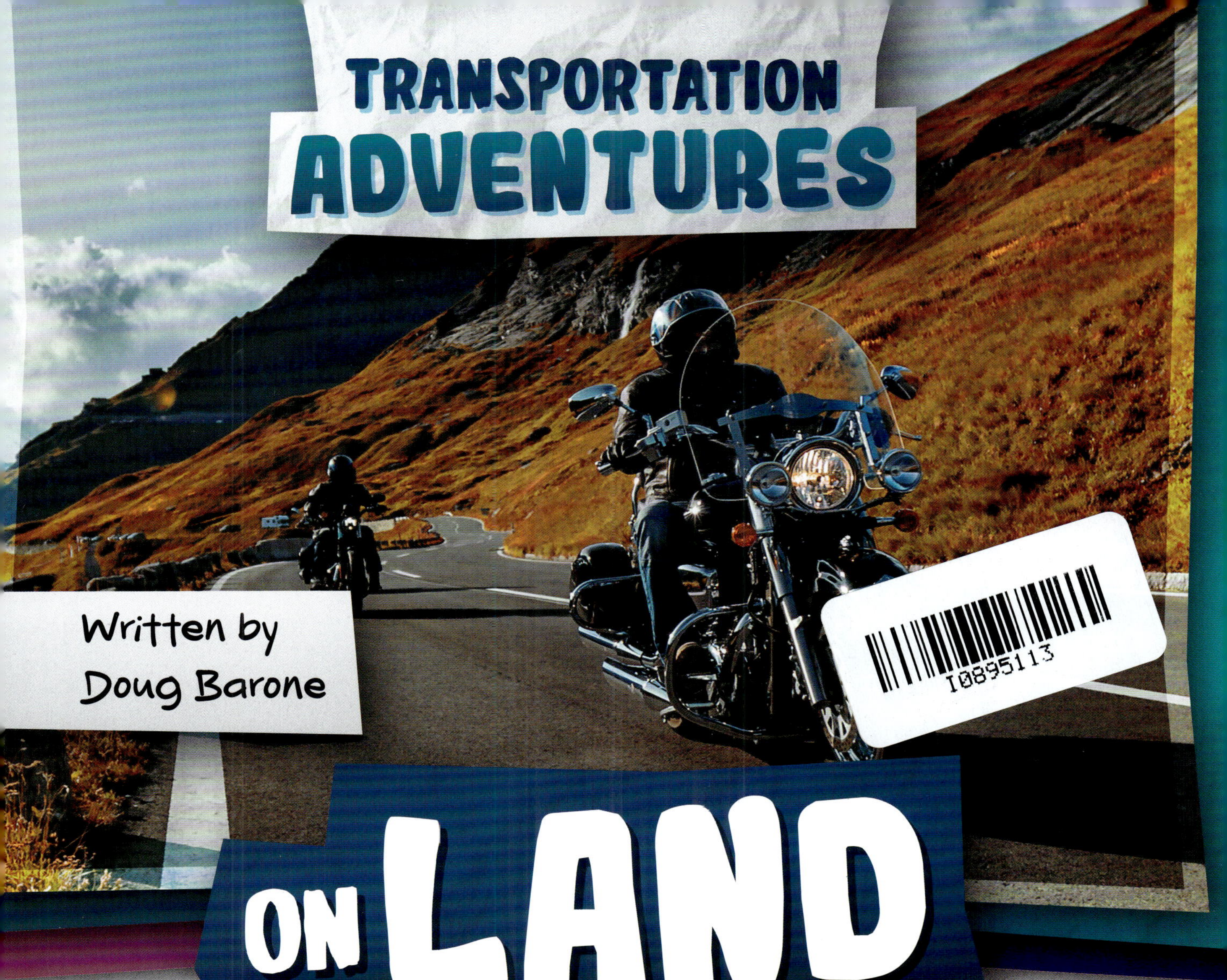

Written by
Doug Barone

ON LAND

KidHaven PUBLISHING

Published in 2027 by
KidHaven Publishing, an Imprint of Greenhaven Publishing, LLC
2544 Clinton St., Buffalo, NY 14224

Written by: Doug Barone
Edited by: Rebecca Phillips-Bartlett
Designed by: Ker Ker Lee

Cataloging-in-Publication Data
Names: Barone, Doug.
Title: On land / Doug Barone.
Description: Buffalo, NY : KidHaven Publishing, 2027. | Series: Transportation adventures | Includes glossary and index.
Identifiers: ISBN 9781534569683 (pbk.) | ISBN 9781534569690 (library bound) | ISBN 9781534569706 (ebook)
Subjects: LCSH: Vehicles--Juvenile literature. | Automobiles--Juvenile literature. | Transportation--Juvenile literature.
Classification: LCC TL147.B376 2027 | DDC 629.222--dc23

Printed in China

CPSIA compliance information: Batch #QS27KH: For further information contact Greenhaven Publishing LLC at 1-844-317-7404.

Please visit our website, www.greenhavenpublishing.com.
For a free color catalog of all our high-quality books,
call toll free 1-844-317-7404
or fax 1-844-317-7405.

Find us on

Photo Credits – Images courtesy of Shutterstock.com, unless otherwise stated.

Cover & Recurring – Lukas Gojda, SoomO2020. 2–3 – Pandora Pictures. 4–5 – Mostovyi Sergii Igorevich, Monkey Business Images. 6–7 – Felix Friebe, Wasu Watcharadachaphong. 8–9 – Gertan, Marzolino. 10–11 – Scott Mattock, Jimmy Kamballur. 12–13 – HodagMedia, Denis Doronin, Halfpoint. 14–15 – PHOTOGRAPHY IS ON, Debu55y, Halfpoint. 16–17 – Sanket27. 18–19 – TAudio und werbung, Wladyslaw, CC BY-SA 2.0 DE, via Wikimedia Commons. 20–21 – Frame Stock Footage, Scharfsinn. 22–23 – Armando Oliveira, Monkey Business Images.

CONTENTS

Words that look like this can be found in the glossary on page 24.

A NEW ADVENTURE!

Transportation is how people get from one place to another. Some modes of transportation are very fast. Others are slower. All kinds can take you on an adventure.

ON LAND

Lots of types of transportation move across the land. Even walking is a type of land transportation. Do you walk to many places? Or do you use other vehicles?

ANIMALS

Thousands of years ago, humans walked everywhere. Then, humans learned that they could travel by riding on animals.

Humans first started riding horses around 4000 BCE.

BCE means Before Common Era. This is the time before the year 0.

Many people still ride animals. In different parts of the world, people ride different kinds of animals. Many people enjoy riding horses. People also ride on camels and elephants.

HORSE-DRAWN CARRIAGES

One of the earliest wheels was invented in Mesopotamia around 3500 BCE.

This important invention helped people make their adventures with animals even easier.

Mesopotamia is now parts of Iraq, Kuwait, Türkiye, and Syria.

Horses are very strong. Humans built vehicles with wheels that horses could pull.

Horse-drawn carts and carriages allowed people to transport more items. Horse-drawn carriages also made journeys more comfortable for people.

TRAINS

Around 1712, steam engines were invented.

Steam engines led to the invention of trains. Trains became popular in the 1820s.

Over time, train engines started using different types of fuel.

Have you ridden on a train before?

Trains travel along tracks that are laid across the ground. Trains stop at stations to let people get on and off.

BICYCLES

Some of the first bicycles were invented in the 1800s.

Velocipedes were early wooden bicycles. They did not have pedals. Penny-farthings are bicycles with a large front wheel and small back wheel.

A bicycle is a great way to go on an adventure. Bicycles use pedals to spin their wheels and move forward.

Adventuring on a bicycle can be a lot of fun. Just remember to wear your helmet!

TRAMS

Trams transport people around towns and cities. Trams follow tracks built into roads.

Early trams were pulled by horses. The first street tram in the United States opened in New York City in 1832.

Some trams were pulled along by long cables. This was very helpful for places with steep hills.

Today, most trams are powered by electricity. They are powered by electrical wires that hang above the road.

CARS

The first practical car was made in 1885 by Karl Benz. It used an internal combustion engine. An internal combustion engine sits inside a vehicle and burns fuel to make power.

Cars became more popular in the 1900s. In 1913, Henry Ford opened the first moving assembly line. This made building a car much faster. It also made cars cheaper for people to buy.

MOTORCYCLES

In 1885, two inventors in Germany put a gas engine on a bicycle. It was the first motorcycle ever made. It had a wooden frame and could be steered.

Motorcycles can come in all different shapes and sizes. Some are built for speed. Some are built to cruise on an adventure.

Motorcycle riders need to wear protective gear to stay safe.

THE FUTURE

The way people travel on land has changed a lot over the years.

Inventors, scientists, and engineers today are still working on new ways to travel across the land.

Inventors are working on driverless cars. These cars use computers to drive and react to things on the road.

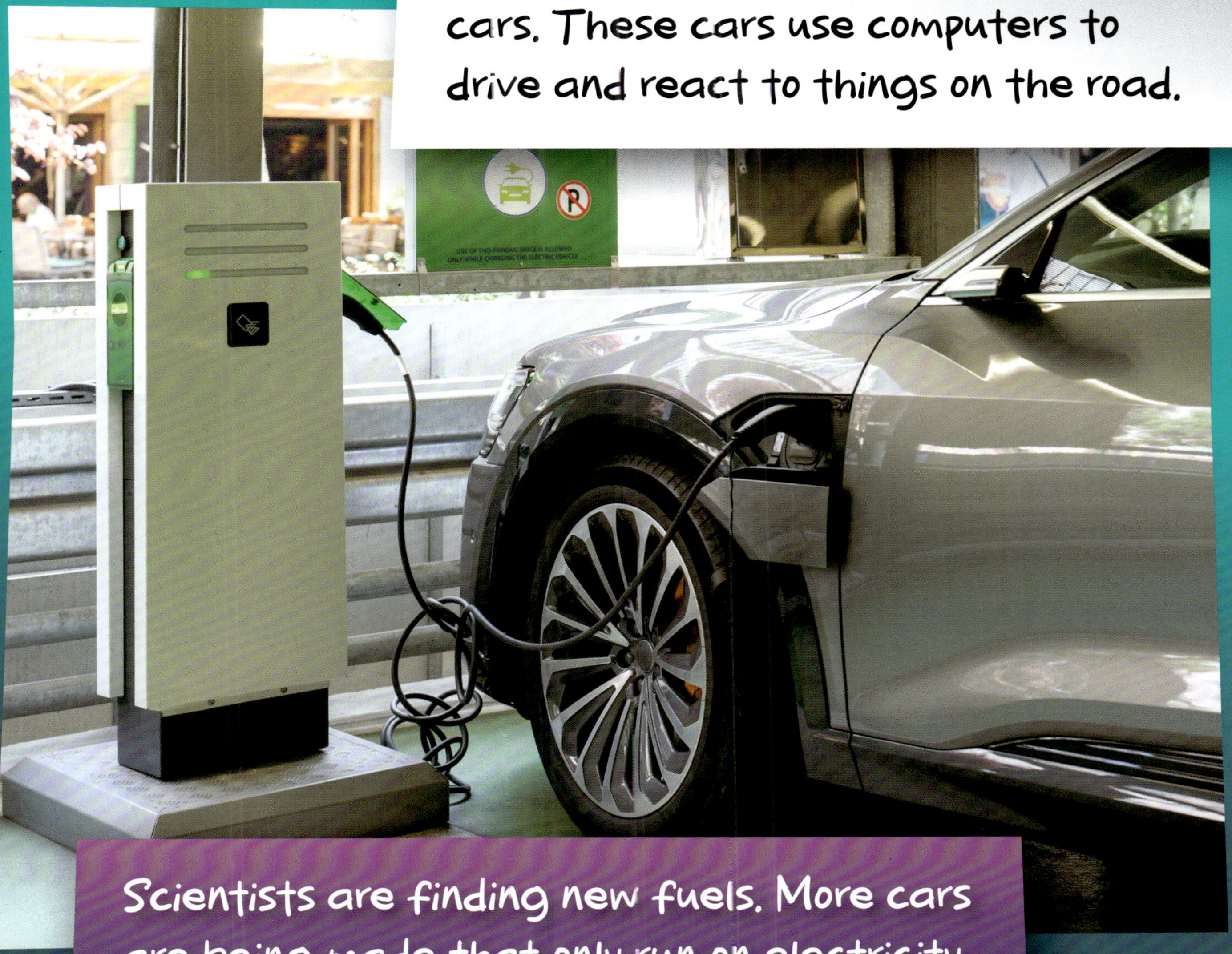

Scientists are finding new fuels. More cars are being made that only run on electricity.

TRANSPORTATION ADVENTURES

There are many different forms of transportation to move across the land. Humans have gone from walking to not even needing a driver for their car!

All these different modes of transportation can be used to go on an adventure. Which ones have you already ridden in? Which ones do you want to ride for your next adventure?

GLOSSARY

assembly putting things together

fuel something that can be used to make energy or power something

invented when something new was made

steam engines machines that use the gas made from heating water to power things

vehicles machines that are used to carry people or things

INDEX